And Time Began

Eugene J. McCarthy

Photo from the Myron Hall Collection
at the Stearns County Historical Society
St. Cloud, Minnesota

Published
By
Lone Oak Press
304 Eleventh Avenue Southeast
Rochester, Minnesota 55904

These poems were originally published in a hard cover
private edition of 1200 numbered copies on December 23,
1968. This publication by Lone Oak Press makes the
poems generally available for the first time.

Photography
by
Larry W. Schwarm

ISBN 0-9627860-6-3
Library of Congress
Catalog Card Number: 93 – 077294

AND TIME BEGAN

by

Eugene J. McCarthy

FOREWARD
by
Donal Heffernan

Eugene McCarthy's love for America has blessed us with political hope, and as a poet, his fine poetry provides a nourishment for our imaginations; poetry's critical role in a culture.

Knowing the Romans, according to Joseph Brodsky, "Means reading the Roman poets, they are the true scribes of their time." Knowing the new America means reading Gene. McCarthy captures our essence in this sometimes rough transition of this latter part of our 20th century, parts he has sheparded as U.S Senator, presidential candidate, and poet. All too rare are poets from industry or from government such as McCarthy, Vaclav Havel and Mario Vargas Lloss: weaving, as William Carlos Williams did, the work of the day into a night of poetry ... "all one, really."

Free-lancing one's destiny with the voters is not an easy road; and the historical impact of it is felt in the wonderful poems that one would expect in Ireland where poetry is a natural part of the day. If Bloom had his day in Dublin, given to him by Joyce,

then McCarthy has many like Bloom here in America,
and McCarthy's eye for detail is as good as Bloom's.
You'll see when you read these poems, such as the
one titled "Three Bad Signs: "Foreverness does not
come easily/The rates should be higher."

Donal Heffernan is the author of "Hillsides," a book of
poetry published by Lone Oak Press (1990). In 1968 he
worked for McCarthy's U.S. presidential campaign in
South Dakota, Wisconsin, Nebraska, Montana, Iowa and
Minnesota

Contents

TO ROBERT LOWELL   11

JUMPING SHIP   13

THREE BAD SIGNS   17

LAMENT OF AN AGING POLITICIAN   22

COMMUNION   24

EQUINOX, SEPTEMBER 1967   27

MARCH EQUINOX 1968   29

RAPID CITY   32

THE HERON   34

THE DAY TIME BEGAN   37

TO ROBERT LOWELL

Poet of purity and of parsimony
using one sense at a time, sparingly.
salt-bleaching white the whiteness of light,
straining the hemp, not nylon line,
scraping the wood to bare the silk grain,

searching in attics and sheds,
of life, salvaging shards and scraps,
of truth, parts of dead poets
pieces of gods.

Myopic, in storms, you cross
the bridge of the faulted rocks
double agent of doubt, smuggler of truth.

Poet-Priest of the bitter sacrament,

what is behind the door in man's house,
what is beneath the cross in God's house?
Look through your less dark glass,
daring as much for man as for God.

Wherever I travel Greece keeps wounding me.
They call the ship which travels Agony 937.
George Seferis

JUMPING SHIP

I signed on the Constitution
for 67 days, 46 ports
a good ship
with wall to wall carpets
clean, with Goren for bridge,
full of joy and forgetfulness
according to Isbrandtsen,
more than seaworthy.

Ignoring the Atlantic waves
nodding to the swells off Africa
somewhat too large
for the Mediterranean,
certainly for the Aegean,
drawing too much for the pier,
we stood off the coast.

Out of your land
from the ship *Agony 937*

out of your language, in translation
you boarded violently,
crying of Greece, George Seferis.

With the wounds of Greece
you have wounded us.
You have wounded us with the deep sound
of women crying out of centuries,
and with the shallow silence
of the buried reed.

You have wounded us with the sharp fear
of the broken oar, marking the grave
on the shore
and with the blunt despair
of the harbors without ships.

You have wounded us with the white
of the almond trees
and with the black
of the burnt out villages.

You have wounded us with the sweetness
of the pomegranate

and with the bitterness
of the salt sea.

You have wounded us
with the weightless walking of children
and with the heaviness of the marble heads
and of the great stones.

You have wounded us unto death
and unto life.

With eleven ports to go
I am jumping ship
to sign on *Agony 937.*

THREE BAD SIGNS

The first Bad Sign is this:
"Green River Ordinance Enforced Here.
Peddlers Not Allowed. "

This is a clean, safe town.
No one can just come round
With ribbons and bright threads
Or new books to be read.
This is an established place.
We have accepted patterns in lace,
And ban itinerant vendors of new forms
                  and whirls,
All things that turn the heads of girls.
We are not narrow, but we live with care.
Gypsies, hawkers and minstrels are right
                     for a fair.
But transient peddlers, nuisances, we say
From Green River must be kept away.
Traveling preachers, actors with a play,
Can pass through, but may not stay.
Phoenicians, Jews, men of Venice -
Know that this is the home of Kiwanis.

All you who have been round the world
                                    to find
Beauty in small things: read our sign
And move on.

The second Bad Sign is this:
"Mixed Drinks."

"Mixed Drinks."
What mystery blinks
As in the thin blood of the neon sign
The uncertain hearts of the customers
Are tested there in the window.
Embolism after embolism, repeating.
Mixed drinks between the art movie
And the Reasonable Rates Hotel.
Mixed drinks are class,
Each requires a different glass.
Mixed drink is manhattan red
Between the adult movie and the
                                unmade bed
Mixed drink is daiquiri green
Between the gospel mission and the sheen

Of hair oil on the rose planted paper.
Mixed drink is forgiveness
Between the vicarious sin
And the half-empty bottle of gin.
Mixed drink is remembrance between
                              unshaded
40-watt bulbs hung from the ceiling,
Between the light a man cannot live by,
And the better darkness.
Mixed drink is the sign of contradiction.

The third Bad Sign is this:
"We Serve All Faiths."

We serve all faiths:
We the morticians.
Tobias is out, he has had it.
We do not bury the dead.
Not, He died, was buried and after three
                              days arose.
But He died, was revived, and after three
                              days was buried alive.
This is our scripture.

Do not disturb the established practitioner.
Do not disturb the traditional mortician:
Giving fans to the church, for hot days,
Dropping a calendar at the nursing home,
A pamphlet in the hospital waiting room,
An ad in the testimonial brochure at the
                                    retirement banquet.
Promising the right music, the artificial grass.
We bury faith of all kinds.
Foreverness does not come easily.
The rates should be higher.

LAMENT OF AN AGING POLITICIAN

The Dream of Gerontion is
                        my dream
and Lowell's self-salted
night sweat, wet, flannel,
                        my morning's
shoulder shroud.

Now, far-sighted I see the distant
                             danger
beyond the coffin confines of
                            telephone booths,
my arms stretch to read, in vain.

Stubbornness and penicillin hold
the aged above me.
My metaphors grow cold and old,
my enemies, both young and bold.

I have left Act I, for involution
and Act II. There mired in
                          complexity
I cannot write Act III.

COMMUNION

Gentle the deer with solicitude
Solace them with salt
Comfort them with apples
Prepare them for the rectitude
Of Man who will come
A stranger with the unfamiliar gun.
The watcher calls. In trust the head
                                    turns
Between the antlers St. Hubert's cross
                                    burns.

No conversion today – but quick shot.
The buck falls to his knees
In decent genuflection to death.
                         The doe flees.
He is not dead. He will arise.
In three weeks, the head
Will look from the wall
But with changed eyes.

But what of the body of swiftness
And litheness. Oh. Witness
Ground heart and muscle

Intestinal cased, tied with gristle,
The sausage sacrament of communion.
So that all may be one
Under the transplanted eyes
         of the watcher.

EQUINOX, SEPTEMBER 1967

Summer ended Friday
at midnight in doubt
between rain and fog
half way through the equinox.

The great wheel of the seasons
had risen to apogee
and stood in balance
defying time's gasping forward pull.

Like a bird held
by hard winds
or a movie reversed
it fell back toward spring.

But then came over, slowly
down falling, inexorable
on the side of autumn
its force against me.

I called. You did not come.
The winter will be longer.

MARCH EQUINOX 1968

Whose foot is on the treadle
That turns the burning stars
Has spun the whole world half way round
Since last I called
Come down. Come down.

The stars that in September
Looked through the mournful rain
Now set their sight again
Upon a world half night, half light.

Men of distant years have said
That much depends on change of seasons
On solstices and equinox
And they have given reasons.

I disagree.
Too much turns on inadvertence
Or what seems to be
An accident of hand or knee
A chance sunrise
A glance of eyes

Whether the wind blows
Which way the river flows
And on other things that come and go
Without regard for season
Or for reason.

But just in case
They may be right,
On this strange night
That marks the end of winter's fall
For lifting help towards spring
Again, to you, I call.

RAPID CITY

Sumac singed in the slant
sun, tumble-weed and thistle, scant
green gone, in the fear of old
thigh bones, brittle in cold.
On every hill a last Indian sits
looking straight west, through saffron slits,
reading his blood, paler and paler, exile,
while parched snakes wait for the first
thin dew to slake their day old thirst.
The coyote cries in the sudden night
and from stars dead a million years, light,
on the yellow leaves of cotton-wood, shows
that under the iron bridge
        a black river is, and flows.

THE HERON

The heron comes before the light
Has quite distinguished day from night.
Where he stands all things turn gray.
His yellow eye rebukes the sun.
Pricked by his beak, all colors run
Through his one leg into the bay.
All day, disdained, the dismal fishes swim
About that one deceiving reed
And flaunt the warning line
That runs from his sun-moved shadow
To the point of death.

Why does the heron wait
Alone, controlled, celibate?
Simon Stylites on his rod
Looking for the weakening of God
The executioner who prays
A day before he slays.
When at last the sun slanted
Beneath his clouded breast has changed
All things to gold, delayed,
The answer comes.

The heron strikes and kills his wish.
For he eats only golden fish.
And that same fish, mirrored
In the heron's avid eyes
Sees himself as golden and dies
in that belief. Both fish and bird
By the same sun, at end betrayed.

THE DAY TIME BEGAN

Our days were yellow and green.
we marked the seasons with respect,
but spring was ours. We were shoots
and sprouts, and greenings.
We heard the first word
that fish were running in the creek.
Secretive we went with men into sheds
for torches and tridents
for nets and traps.
We shared the wildness of that week,
in men and fish. First fruits
after the winter. Dried meat gone,
the pork barrel holding only brine.
Bank clerks came out in skins,
teachers in loin clouts,
while game wardens drove
                    in darkened cars,
watching the vagrant flares
beside the fish mad streams, or crouched
at home to see who came and went,
holding their peace,
surprised by violence.

We were spendthrift of time.
A day was not too much to spend
to find a willow right for a whistle
to blow the greenest sound the world
has ever heard.
Another day to search the oak and
                              hickory thickets,
geometry and experience run together
to choose the fork, fit
for a sling.
Whole days long we pursued the
                              spotted frogs
and dared the curse of newts and toads.
New adams, unhurried, pure, we checked
                              the names
given by the old.
Some things we found well titled
blood-root for sight
skunks for smell
crab apples for taste
yarrow for sound
mallow for touch.
Some we found named ill, too little
                              or too much

or in a foreign tongue.
These we challenged with new names.

Space was our preoccupation,
infinity, not eternity our concern.
We were strong bent on counting,
the railroad ties, so many to a mile,
the telephone poles, the cars that passed,
marking our growth against
                            the door frames.

The sky was a kite,
I flew it on a string, winding
it in to see its blue, again
to count the whirling swallows,
and read the patterned scroll of
                            blackbirds turning,
to check the markings of the hawk,
and then letting it out to the end
of the last pinched inch of
string, in the vise of thumb and finger.

One day the string broke.
The kite fled over the shoulder of the world,

but reluctantly, reaching back
                         in geat lunges
as lost kites do, or as a girl running
in a reversed movie, as at each
                         arched step, the earth
set free, leaps forward, catching
her farther back,
the treadmill doubly betraying,
remote and more remote.

Now I lie on a west facing hill in October.
The dragging string having circled
                         the world, the universe,
crosses my hand in the grass. I do not
                                    grasp it.
It brushes my closed eyes, I do not open.
That world is no longer mine,
                         but for remembrance.
Space ended then, and time began.

Colophon

"And Time Began" was designed, edited and typeset
at
Lone Oak Press
by Ray Howe
Editor & Publisher.

The book was composed in Microsoft Word for Windows,
scans were done on a Microtek 600Z with OmniPage
Professional. The font used is Windsor, from Laser
Master and the type set on a LaserMaster LX6

The Photography
by
Larry Schwarm

"I photograph the land ... subjects basic to my soul. I grew up close to the land and it became a reference to the way that I see ...
My childhood was spent in a part of the counry where the horizon is level for 360 degrees and a tree is a landmark. A landscape that is very subtle. I search for rare situations when elements come together in significant ways. I look for the sublime."

Larry Schwarm teaches photography at Emporia State University in Kansas. Photography has been his passion for the last 20 years. Always an artist, he has also been a commercial photographer in Milwaukee and a staff photographer at the Kansas University Art Museum. His work has been published and exhibited extensively, including traveling exhibitions by the National Museum of American Art/Smithsonian Institution.

Photo from the Myron Hall Collection at the Stearns County, Minnesota, Historical Society.